50

I is for Island

A Prince Edward Island Alphabet

Written by Hugh MacDonald and Illustrated by Brenda Jones

Sleeping Bear Press˜

315 E. Eisenhower Parkway, Suite 200
Ann Arbor, MI 48108
www.sleepingbearpress.com

Sleeping Bear Press is an imprint of Gale, a part of Cengage Learning.

Printed and bound in the United States.

10 9 8 7 6 5 4 3 2 1

Library of Congress Cataloging-in-Publication Data

MacDonald, Hugh, 1945-
I is for island : a Prince Edward Island alphabet / Hugh MacDonald ;
Brenda Jones.
p. cm.
ISBN 978-1-58536-367-4
1. Prince Edward Island—Juvenile literature. 2. Alphabet books—
Juvenile literature. I. Jones, Brenda, 1953- ill. II. Title.
F1047.4.M35 2012
971.7—dc23   2011039170

To Adam, Matthew, Melody, Andrew, Allister, and David

DAD

*To my peaceful Island home, its inspirational landscapes,
and the people who have taught me to appreciate them.*

BRENDA

A is for *Abegweit*,
Isle cradled on the sea,
the Mi'kmaq first loved it,
each clam and bird and tree.

Abegweit is the name the Mi'kmaq people gave Prince Edward Island. It means "cradled on the waves." The Mi'kmaq were the first people known to inhabit PEI. They are descendants of the first indigenous people who lived here 10,500 years ago. Living off the island's abundant natural resources, the Mi'kmaq people were a great help to European settlers who later settled here.

The Mi'kmaq people believe that family and gatherings are very important and nowadays their cultural and spiritual ceremonies add richness to many events throughout the year. They, along with representatives of other tribal groups from across Canada and the U.S., gather and celebrate at annual powwows on Lennox Island and Panmure Island. Every year Islanders and visitors from around the world are treated to a colourful demonstration of native dancing and music, culture, and crafts.

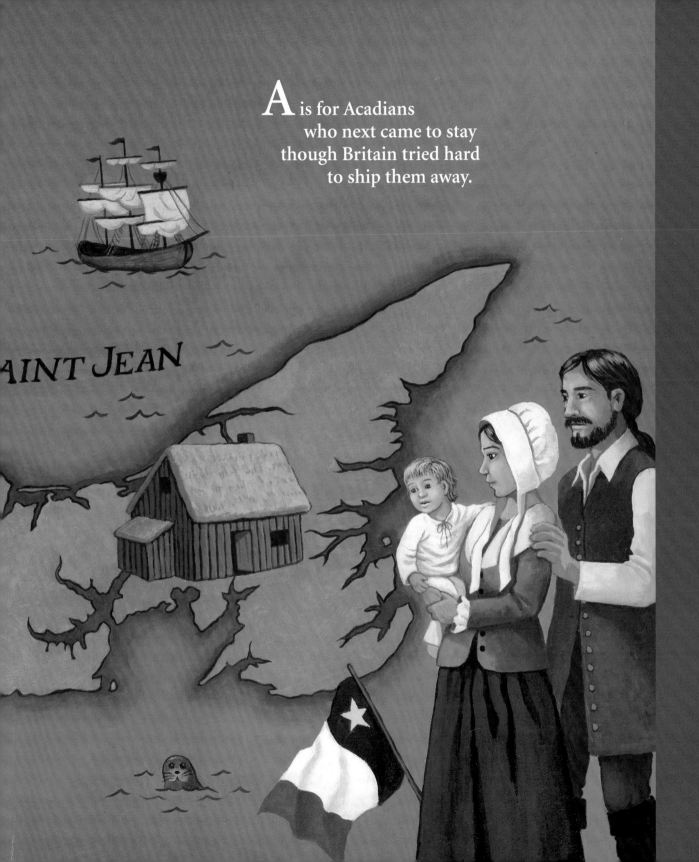

A is for Acadians
who next came to stay
though Britain tried hard
to ship them away.

Island Acadians are descended from French adventurers and explorers who settled mainly in what is now known as Nova Scotia. They created a land of their own which they named Acadia (in French *Acadie*). Acadians began to arrive on Isle Saint Jean (PEI) in 1720, drawn here by the island's plentiful harvests and wanting to flee troubles on the mainland.

Living conditions for the new arrivals proved dismal and many suffered greatly. After the English took over the island in 1758, about 3,000 Acadians were deported and their livestock taken away. By 1768, 203 Acadians who had escaped deportation lived on the island. Most Acadians living on PEI today descended from this group. Many place names are English versions of French names, or direct translations. For example: *Bedec* became Bedeque and *Rivière du Nord* became North River.

Bb

Due to the pounding of the incoming tides, the sandstone under PEI breaks down into fine silicone-laden reddish sand. It sometimes bleaches out to almost white. But the same natural forces that create lovely sand beaches are also continually eroding the surrounding shoreline. Storms and tidal surges can tear away dunes and great chunks of land. Weathering, the effects of freezing and thawing and precipitation, also breaks down the island's underlying sandstone into sand.

The ecosystem of the shoreline is delicate. Marram grass (beach grass) can bind giant sand dunes together, helping hold sand in place, but will not stand up to human foot traffic or storm surges. The piping plover is an endangered species that nests on beaches. Great care is taken to protect these nesting areas. Beaches are beautiful places but require the cooperation of visitors in order to survive. PEI has hundreds of these beaches where it is possible to swim and play or stroll for hours without meeting another human being.

B is for our varied Beaches,
     on our rivers and our coast.
And the summer sun that bleaches
     silky sand that's warm as toast.

Charlottetown, our capital city, was incorporated in 1855 and named after Queen Charlotte, wife of King George III. It has been called "the Cradle of Confederation." In 1864 PEI, Nova Scotia, and New Brunswick were British colonies. A meeting held in Charlottetown to talk about uniting the colonies was attended by politicians from other British colonies in North America. As a result of the meeting the new Dominion of Canada was formed in 1867. PEI later joined in 1873.

PEI has three counties: Prince, Queens, and Kings. They are represented as three saplings on the provincial flag. Other elements on the flag are: the gold lion (Prince Edward); green grass (symbolizing England and PEI); and a large oak tree (the provincial tree).

Today Charlottetown is a vibrant city full of parks and many attractions, including the Confederation Centre of the Arts. It was presented as a gift by the 10 Provincial Governments and the Federal Government to celebrate the 100th anniversary of the Charlottetown Conference. The Centre's space includes a theatre, art gallery, museum, and library.

Charlottetown also has a fine example of one of the many important buildings from architect William Harris. St. Paul's Anglican Church was built in 1896. There are a number of historic churches found on PEI.

C is for Charlottetown,
    the Cradle of Confederation.
Here in 1864
    was born a proud new nation.

An elegant Queen Anne Revival structure, Dalvay-By-the Sea was originally built in 1896 as a family home for Alexander MacDonald, a Scottish-American oil baron. Its construction was supervised by Charlottetown architect Charles Chappell, using mostly local materials. Queen Anne Revival-style buildings have lots of bays, gables, and dormers and use a variety of colours and textures.

Dalvay-By-the-Sea had several owners between 1930 and 1937. It was bought by the Government of Canada in 1937 to become part of the Prince Edward Island National Park. Since that time it has been operated as a resort hotel, offering its guests elegant dining and accommodations. It is now a National Historic site.

D
d

D is for Dalvay-By-the-Sea,
a house with Island history.
Built in Queen Anne Revival style,
it served one family for a while.

E e

E is for the stalwart East Point Light
whose beacon flashes day and night.
Its light a steady sure support
in guiding sailors back to port.

There are dozens of lighthouses all along the coast of PEI but the East Point Lighthouse is probably the most popular. Built in 1867, it is located on the easternmost point of the island. Visitors are welcome to climb to the top to look out to sea or across the land. Open from June 16 to Labour Day, the East Point Lighthouse attracts hundreds of visitors every year.

Lighthouses can be identified by the way they are painted, their patterns and colours, and the number and timing of their light flashes. Before 1873, when big trees and large pieces of lumber were plentiful, lighthouses were eight-sided. After that date, shipbuilding used up much of the larger wood, and lighthouses were built as squares that got smaller and smaller as they got nearer the top. Lighthouses were originally built to warn ships and boats about dangerous reefs and tides; however, new navigational systems have taken over that role. But people still love these beautiful buildings, which continue to attract photographers and visitors from all over the world.

F is for Ferries that sail to and fro
and take us to places we all want to go.
A trip on a ferry is a delightful cruise—
sit and relax, do whatever you choose.

Ferries have been part of PEI life for almost 100 years. The first ferry services began in order to shorten travel between nearby towns and villages separated by bays and rivers. Up until 1917 manned ice boats carried mail, cargo, and passengers to the island from the mainland across the heavy winter ice. In 1917 a ferry crossing was established to operate between Borden and Cape Tormentine, New Brunswick. Later ferry services were also set up to cross between the towns of Souris and *Cap-aux Meules* in the Magdalen Islands, Quebec, and between Wood Island and Caribou, Nova Scotia in 1941.

With the opening of the Confederation Bridge in 1997 connecting PEI and New Brunswick, the ferry service between Borden and Cape Tormentine was cancelled. Northumberland Ferries continue to operate seasonally between Wood Island and Caribou, and ferries now cross year-round between Souris and the Magdalen Islands, Quebec.

Gg

Prince Edward Island has had several names over the centuries, including *Abegweit* and Saint John's Isle (Île Saint-Jean). Its unofficial names, the Garden Province and the Million-Acre Farm, reflect its natural beauty and fertile farmland. The colours red and green are everywhere, from plowed fields to lush lawns to the island's forests, which contain a wide variety of trees, including oak, spruces, balsam fir, red maple and sugar maple, aspen, white birch, beech, and yellow birch.

The provincial flower is the stemless lady's slipper (*Cypripedium acaule*). It gets its name from the shape of its petals. Adopted as the official flower in 1947, its blossom is usually pink in colour but sometimes white. Picking them is discouraged.

At approximately 5,660 square kilometres, PEI is the smallest Canadian province. Yet it is the most densely populated with more than 145,000 people. It was named for Prince Edward, Duke of Kent and Strathern, son of King George III and the father of Queen Victoria.

G is for the Garden Province,
a lovely isle that's lush and green.
Each tidy house and barn and fence
all painted up so neat and clean.

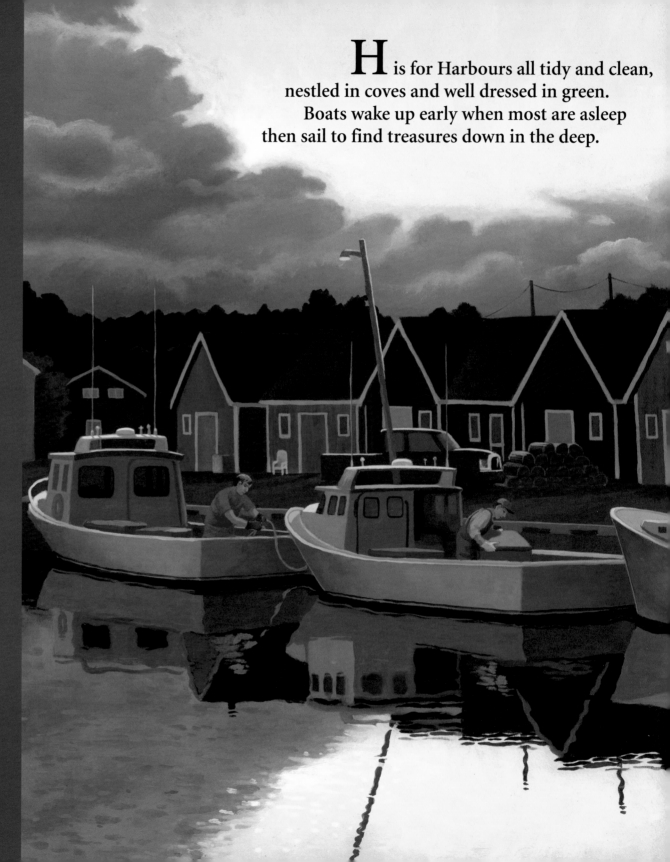

H h

His for Harbours all tidy and clean,
nestled in coves and well dressed in green.
Boats wake up early when most are asleep
then sail to find treasures down in the deep.

PEI's dozens of harbours are busy places during fishing season and a favourite stopping place for the many photographers and tourists who visit the Island. Lobster setting day in North Rustico and the other lobster harbours is an exciting day where everyone rises early to see the trap-laden boats head out to sea. Ports like Covehead Harbour have fishermen who add to their fishing income by offering their boats and skills to people who would like to experience deep-sea fishing. Montague, Charlottetown, Summerside, Souris, and other ports operate marina services for visiting boats. At North Lake visitors can try fishing for giant bluefin tuna.

Community harbours are bustling places. There are frequent suppers and socials in church halls as well as those held by clubs and other organizations. These harbours are one of PEI's most important attractions for tourism, and their processing factories and small businesses help keep surrounding communities alive.

Every day, all over the Island, indoors and out, thousands of people are enjoying winter sports. The PEI Sports Hall of Fame lists almost 50 sports that are played here. The most popular is hockey. While PEI may have the population of a small Ontario town, it has the highest number of hockey rinks per capita in the country.

At least 30 Islanders have played or are presently playing in the National Hockey League. No other place in Canada with such a small population has produced as many fine hockey players. Brad Richards led Tampa Bay to a Stanley Cup and he won the Conn Smythe and Lady Byng Trophy. Adam McQuaid helped Boston win the Stanley Cup, too. Other well-known players include Dave Cameron, John Chabot, Gerard Gallant, and Forbie Kennedy.

I is for the island's Ice and snow,
the heart of the winter we love so.
To ski or skate or to walk or slide,
just for the joy of being outside.

I i

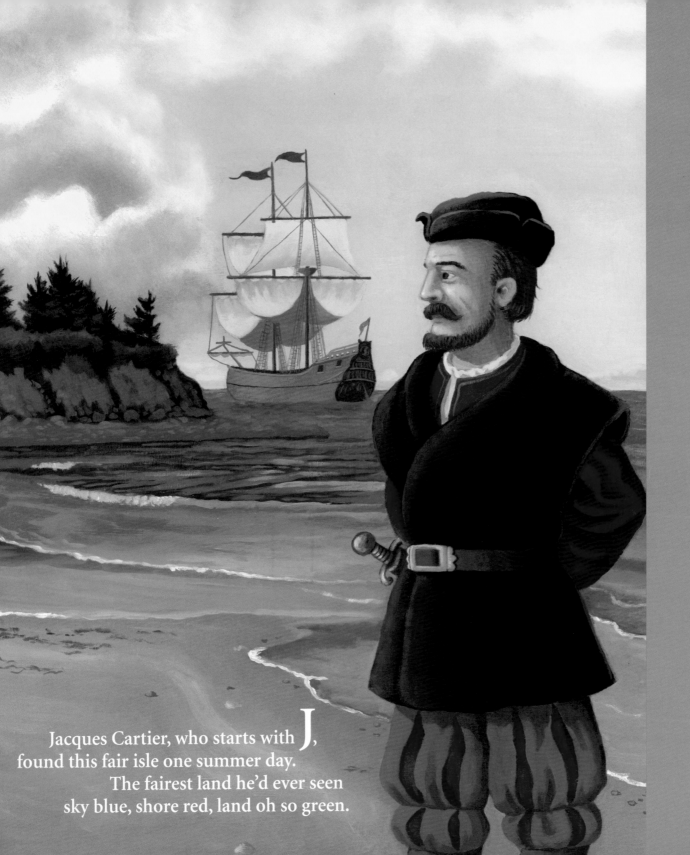

Jj

Jacques Cartier, who starts with J,
found this fair isle one summer day.
The fairest land he'd ever seen
sky blue, shore red, land oh so green.

In 1534 Jacques Cartier was sent by King Francis I of France to search for a better passage to the riches of India and East Asia. He sailed north across the Atlantic and entered the Gulf of St. Lawrence through the Strait of Belle Isle that passes between what is now western Newfoundland and eastern Labrador. Cartier is usually given credit for the "discovery" of Canada despite evidence of previous voyages by the Vikings. His journey took him past what are now the Magdalen Islands and PEI. He is considered to be the first white man to land on Prince Edward Island. He wrote in his ship's log that it was "the fairest land 'tis possible to see."

Cartier didn't find the passage he sought, but encountered a number of Mi'kmaq, and later, Iroquois from whom he learned of the St. Lawrence River. He returned to France without further exploration due to the approach of winter, taking two Iroquois as guests, and determined to make a second voyage of exploration the following year.

K is for Kayak, a swift gliding craft,
or you might like to swim from a raft.
The Isle is criss-crossed by rivers and streams,
more than enough for all of your dreams.

No one on Prince Edward Island is ever far from a river. There are within the island's 224-kilometre length, almost 100 named rivers. Most are not, strictly speaking, rivers but instead are large streams filled with saltwater that flows in from the Gulf of St. Lawrence or Northumberland Strait and then mixes with a small amount of freshwater from the land.

Kayakers or canoeists travel past a wide variety of plants and animals, as well as lots of camping spots and fishing holes. There are plenty of waterfowl, shore birds and sea birds, and, perched on surrounding tree branches, birds like the blue jay (*Cyanocitta cristata*), which is the provincial bird. Near the coastline, adjacent salt marshes team with life, and occasional red-winged blackbirds can be seen.

Many rivers, like the Hillsboro, the Montague, the Mill, the Hunter, the Cardigan, lead to small harbours and thriving communities where boaters can find accommodations, fine dining, shopping, and entertainment.

Kk

L l

L is for Lobster, a true Island treat,
the sweetest shellfish that you'll ever eat.
Fresh from the ocean, then into the pot,
served on a plate, from the shell, piping hot.

There are two lobster seasons in PEI. The first runs in the east through May and June, the second, in the west from mid-August until the beginning of October. Most Island fishers use single-keeled Cape Islander fishing boats with a flat bottom and a deck with a high step up toward the bow.

Traditional Island lobster traps are built by the fishers themselves of wood and twine but other materials are used as well. Traps are baited with flounder, herring, and mackerel. Lobsters climb backward through wooden rings in the knitted heads and, once inside, the larger ones cannot escape. Undersized lobsters can exit through a smaller opening in the parlour of the trap. Careful measurements are made to ensure that lobsters are of legal size.

Setting Day is the most exciting day of the year for fisherfolk and their community. With boats piled high with traps, the crews begin arriving around 4:00 a.m. They race out together at 6:00 a.m. to arrive first at the best fishing grounds.

And don't forget the Island's famous lobster suppers—a well-deserved treat after a long day of fishing!

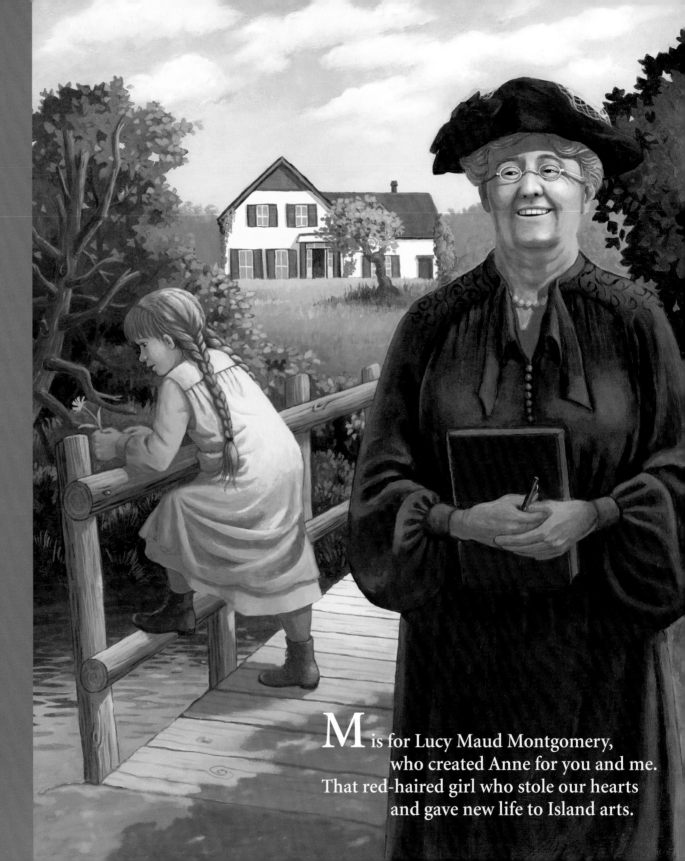

L. M. Montgomery, known to family and friends as Maud, was born in the small community of Clifton (now New London) in 1874. Maud's writings include "The Island Hymn," *Anne of Green Gables* (1908), other Anne books, and many other novels, collections, and anthologies, most set on PEI.

Raised by her grandparents, Maud loved reading, and showed early signs of becoming a writer. She taught school briefly after teacher training, but following her grandfather's death, began to write in earnest. Her powerful, moving stories have been translated into dozens of languages worldwide and her characters, particularly Anne Shirley, the heroine of many of her books, are known and loved worldwide. *Anne of Green Gables*, the musical, has played at Confederation Centre of the Arts' Charlottetown Festival for more than four decades. A sequel, *Anne & Gilbert*, had its first performance at Victoria Playhouse in 2005 and now plays at Harbourfront Theatre in Summerside. The fictional location of Green Gables can be found at Cavendish Beach in Prince Edward Island National Park.

M m

M is for Lucy Maud Montgomery,
who created Anne for you and me.
That red-haired girl who stole our hearts
and gave new life to Island arts.

N n

Prince Edward Island is located in the Gulf of St. Lawrence and is one of four Atlantic Provinces. PEI's three provincial neighbours are: Nova Scotia (to the east and south), New Brunswick (to the west and south), and Newfoundland and Labrador (to the north).

The island is separated from the mainland by the Northumberland Strait, which is a 290-kilometre-long body of water. In 1997 PEI was linked to the New Brunswick mainland by the Confederation Bridge. It is the longest bridge in the world that spans a body of water that freezes solid over the winter months. Spring, summer, and fall, Northumberland Ferries operates a service that connects eastern PEI to Nova Scotia. Islanders must travel to Sydney, NS, for a ferry link to Newfoundland.

The Atlantic Provinces represent that part of Canada first discovered and settled by Europeans.

N is for Neighbours and Northumberland Strait,
people and places we all celebrate.
New Brunswick, Nova Scotia, Newfoundland, PEI—
all bound tightly together by sea, earth, and sky.

O is the first letter of Old Home Week,
that annual break from our workplace care,
when the childhood joys of our summer peak,
and all Islanders rush home for the fair.

Old Home Week is the largest annual fair on PEI, and for many Islanders it is the best week of the year. It has taken place in Charlottetown since 1888. With its midway, fairgrounds, annual exhibition of arts, crafts, and cooking, the fair has grown into a giant celebration of PEI rural life and entertainment. Traditionally, working people from across the Island step away from their farms, their boats, their businesses or their professions to come to the fair.

The fair's attractions have grown over the years, including a midway added in 1914 and harness racing and vaudeville shows added in the 1940s. The festivities finish with the Gold Cup and Saucer Parade that draws thousands of spectators every year. It is a preliminary to the Gold Cup and Saucer Race that is the premier harness racing event in the Maritimes.

P is for Potatoes the pride of Spud Isle,
the spud is a part of Island lifestyle.
Fried, boiled, scalloped, or mashed on your plate,
the smoothest, sweetest thing you ever ate.

PEI accounts for a third of Canada's total potato production. For this reason the province was once called "Spud Island" by many Canadians. The potato, due to its high food value, is the world's fourth largest food crop. Potatoes are high in nutrients, low in fat, and contain a good balance of the eight essential amino acids.

PEI has produced potatoes for export since the late 1770s and the spud is the island's primary cash crop. It brings one billion dollars annually into the province's economy, producing more than 8,000 jobs. And in spite of the fact that it is Canada's smallest province, PEI is the leading potato grower. Over half of these potatoes are used in the processing industry, most turned into frozen potato products distributed across Canada and to almost 30 countries around the world.

PEI potato growers are required to take special training to qualify for licenses to apply pesticides. Precautions must be observed concerning wind direction and speed, and buffer zones established around streams, creeks, and other waterways.

Q

Prince Edward Island seafood is not only available in our restaurants and snack bars; there are many locations around the province where clams and quahogs are there for the taking.

Quahogs are a special North Atlantic shellfish treat that can be harvested along with soft-shell clams along the shores of rivers and bays. You can also visit places like Georgetown and go out to the shallow surrounding waters and gather giant bar clams that make the finest clam chowder you have ever tasted. PEI's seafood is famous outside its borders and our mussels are shipped to markets around the world. PEI's Malpeque oysters are considered the finest available.

Clambakes on beaches around a campfire under a moonlit sky are popular and occur all summer long. In late summer it is common to include fresh-picked buttery corn and there are frequently pots of clams and corn bubbling side by side over an open fire.

Q is for Quahog, a lovely treat,
    there for the taking under your feet.
Clams to be dug from the riverside
    or out on sand bars where big ones hide.

PEI is famous for its colourful and fertile red soil, suitable for growing a wide variety of crops, including potatoes and food grains, garden vegetables, cole crops (such as cabbage, brussels sprouts, broccoli, cauliflower), and beans, like soybeans. Where does the red colour come from? The soil and underlying sandstone rock contain a high iron content which, through contact with oxygen, turns into the distinctive red colour.

Another important "red" is the provincial tree which is the red oak. Adopted as the official tree in 1905, the red oak was commonly seen on the island in its early days but it is less abundant now due to harvesting (it was heavily used in furniture-making and cabinetry) and land-clearing. The red oak can still be found in various places on the island, including Charlottetown's Royalty Oaks Natural Area.

R r

R is for our productive Red soil,
the fertile ground on which farmers toil.
They harvest grains, and beans, taters by the loads,
toting them from fields along red dusty roads.

The waters off PEI, both shallow and deep, have played a very important role in shaping the island and its inhabitants from the arrival of the Mi'kmaq to the present day. Adults and children alike enjoy boating, fishing, or just a day at the beach.

Deep-sea fishing in the Gulf of St. Lawrence and the Northumberland Strait is popular with both Islanders and tourists. From July into September enthusiasts looking to catch mackerel, giant bluefin tuna, and even shark can take advantage of the many charter excursions available from ports such as North Rustico, Covehead Harbour, and others.

S s

S is for the sparkling Sea
where we jump and splash with glee,
fish and swim and play with boats,
build sand castles ringed with moats.

PEI has many opportunities for hiking and cycling. The Confederation Trail is a bicycling/hiking trail that spans the island from east to west. Running more than 270 kilometres from Elmira to Tignish, this system is built on the former Canadian National Railways rail bed, following abandoned railway lines.

National and provincial parks and heritage sites have wonderful trails systems open to the public. PEI has many kilometres of heritage red-clay roads that remain much as they have been for hundreds of years. They pass by woodlands and farm fields shaded by trees along each side. Visitors can park and explore.

PEI's Department of Forestry maintains six woodlots that are open to the public, complete with trails and information on the island's forestry practices. Many communities support and maintain their own walking trails. The Island Trails Web site has information on dozens of trails, including length and difficulty. Island woodlands contain former farm trails and roadways, and most local farmers and landowners are happy to share them, only asking that users leave the property as beautiful as they found it.

T is for Island Trails,
trails beyond compare.
Fun pathways to explore
with mysteries to share.

U is for U-picks where you can pick your own
food that is fresh from the earth where it's grown.
Vegetables, berries still warm from the sun,
where children can learn good nutrition is fun.

Prince Edward Island has been dependent on agriculture for food supply and income since its beginnings. Gradually, as in most places, small family farms have been giving way to larger corporate farm agriculture and many Islanders have moved from the countryside into Charlottetown and Summerside, PEI's two small cities.

Many Islanders continue to grow their own vegetables in backyard gardens, or purchase local agriculture products at farmer's markets or grocery stores. Many others continue to bottle their own jams and jellies. Visits to U-picks are popular events and the island has hundreds, supplying strawberries, red and black raspberries, blueberries, blackberries, black and red currants, elderberries, and more. Several orchards also offer visitors the chance to pick their own apples, plums, or pears. Some farms have U-picks where you can pick your own vegetables.

And there are Christmas tree farms where customers can have the pleasure and excitement of selecting and cutting down their own fir or pine tree to decorate their homes over the Christmas season.

Uu

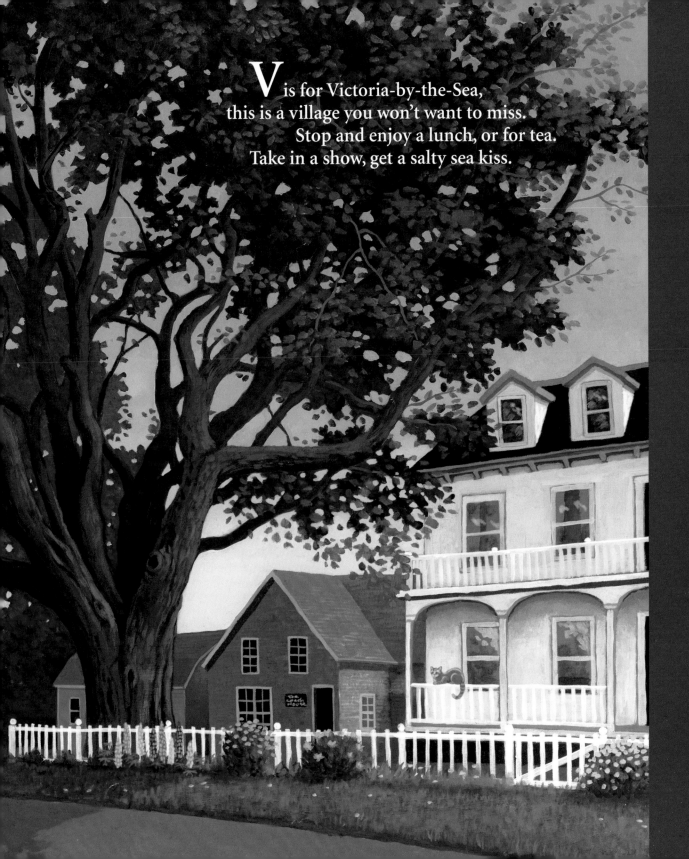

V is for Victoria-by-the-Sea,
this is a village you won't want to miss.
Stop and enjoy a lunch, or for tea.
Take in a show, get a salty sea kiss.

V
v

When visiting Victoria-by-the-Sea it is easy
to imagine you have just entered a storybook.
Located on the south shore of PEI, halfway
between Charlottetown and Summerside,
Victoria was founded in 1819. In the late 1800s,
it was an important and bustling seaport.

While it is a small place with a year-round
population of less than two hundred, the village
is one of PEI's favourite tourist destinations.
Just walking around the tree-lined streets is a
pleasure. There are lovely, unique shops with
books, and crafts, and chocolates. There are
fine dining experiences and there are elegant
tea shops. Special attractions include the
Victoria Playhouse, which offers live theatrical
productions during the summer and the
Victoria Seaport Museum, the second oldest
lighthouse on the island. And there are lovely
places to stay. Best of all are the wonderful,
welcoming people who live there.

The wind filled the sails of the wooden ships that carried the first European settlers to PEI. The wind powered fishing boats as well as the warships of France and Britain. Today PEI waters are alive with the sails of hundreds of modern sailing craft that come seeking adventure, supplies, and shelter in our many rivers, inlets, harbours, and bays.

That same wind brings winter storms and moist cool ocean air in the heat of summer. It now provides a major source of alternate electrical energy from the province's many wind farms with their giant windmills. Approximately 15% of electricity used on the island is generated from renewable energy (largely wind turbines); the provincial government seeks to increase that amount to 50% by 2015.

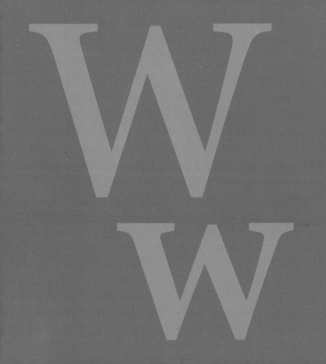

W is for the Winds that blow,
    that drive our island's rain and snow,
that whirl our modern windmills round,
    and sweetly cool the sun-scorched ground.

X marks the spot where the trains once ran,
to carry the cargo, pick up the cream can,
move products and people all around,
roaring and tooting, shaking the ground.

One of the conditions for PEI's entry into Canadian Confederation was that Canada take over the operation of the Prince Edward Island Railway. The island colony didn't join Canada in 1867 because it saw no financial need to do so. By 1872, however, it owed a great deal on the new railroad it had built. The debt was large enough that when Canada agreed to operate the railroad, the colony agreed to join the confederation in 1873. Railroads served the province from 1875 until 1989 when the convenience and speed of highway travel and shipping took business away. When the railroad no longer earned enough money to continue, it was closed down.

For those who still love the old railway system, the Elmira Railway Museum has recreated the former wooden station house, platform, freight shed, and stationmaster's office. There is also a miniature train system that takes visitors around the local area, and a stage for local festivals and events. Elmira is the eastern entry point for the PEI Rails to Trails system.

X
X

Y is for the tragic Yankee Gale,
a wind that sank a hundred ships.
Just one of many a painful tale
of storms and deadly fishing trips.

Yy

Sailors and fishermen know that the same sea that offers rich harvests, enjoyable pastimes, and beautiful settings can also turn deadly. Sudden storms destroyed many ships and took hundreds of lives in the waters around the island over the centuries. And today, despite all the scientific advances and accurate weather predictions, lives are sometimes still lost.

The Yankee Gale took place on October 3, 1851. On that day a violent storm destroyed or stranded nearly 100 fishing boats of the American fishing fleet, killing dozens of fishermen. It was one of the worst fishing disasters in Maritime history. And the storm didn't spare PEI sailors or shippers. Dozens of local vessels were wrecked or lost and local sailors died, including those listed among the crews of the American fishing vessels. Island vessels were washed ashore all over the Atlantic region. And it wasn't the last great storm. There have been several since and there are more to come.

The forces of nature continue to shape PEI, especially its coastline. There is a zigzag look to the island, whether seen from the air, on a road map, or simply as one walks along the beach in the sunshine.

Under the relentless pounding of the waves (either daily surge or from storms) and the effects of freeze and thaw, the red sandstone breaks down into smaller and smaller rocks and eventually fine sand. And while this makes for fine beaches, erosion is a serious problem. Soil erosion happens when particles of soil are loosened and removed. It can be caused by wind as well as water, although for PEI erosion by water is the larger issue. Erosion can cause significant damage, including threatening shoreline property such as the historic West Point Lighthouse.

But soil erosion is not only found on the coastline. It can affect soil inland, especially farmland, due to rainfall and hilly terrain. Conservation efforts to control soil erosion are a high priority on the island.

Z z

The coast of the Island Zigzags around,
up green rivers, harbours, and bays,
while waves lap at its famous red ground,
and make sandy beaches where people play.

Island Q & A

1. What is the name the Mi'kmaq people first gave Prince Edward Island? What does it mean?

2. Who was Charlottetown named after?

3. What type of structure is Dalvay-By-the Sea?

4. What is the name of the bridge that connects PEI to New Brunswick?

5. What is the provincial flower?

6. Who is considered to be the first white man to land on PEI?

7. What famous novel chronicles a young girl's life on PEI and who was its author?

8. What is the name of the body of water that separates PEI from the mainland?

9. What vegetable is the island's primary cash crop?

10. What is the provincial tree?

ANSWERS

1. *Abegweit*—it means "cradled on the waves."

2. Queen Charlotte, wife of King George III

3. Queen Anne Revival

4. Confederation Bridge

5. Stemless lady's slipper

6. Jacques Cartier

7. *Anne of Green Gables* written by Lucy Maud Montgomery

8. Northumberland Strait

9. Potato

10. The red oak

Hugh MacDonald

Poet, editor, and novelist Hugh MacDonald is poet laureate for Prince Edward Island from Jan 1, 2010, until Dec 31, 2012. He is perhaps best known to Islanders as the PEI representative for Random Acts of Poetry, which has brought poetry to the streets and workplaces across Canada. A retired teacher, Mr. MacDonald is a full-time writer. His children's books include *Crosby and Me* and *Chung Lee Loves Lobsters*, which won the L. M. Montgomery Children's Literature Award. In 2004 he was presented with the Award for Distinguished Contribution to the Literary Arts on Prince Edward Island. Mr. MacDonald lives in Brudenell.

Brenda Jones

Brenda Jones grew up on Prince Edward Island, and then moved to Montreal in her early 20s, beginning a career in film animation. For 20 years she worked for private studios, doing colour design, backgrounds, and art direction for many animated television series. Her parallel career as an illustrator began in the '80s after her daughter was born. She has now published more than a dozen books, including *Skunks for Breakfast*, which won the Lillian Shepherd Award for illustration. Ms. Jones recently returned to Prince Edward Island and lives in Charlottetown.